THE RESURRECTION OF JESUS

WORKBOOK

The Credo Courses

THE RESURRECTION OF JESUS: WORKBOOK
© 2014 by Credo Courses, The

ISBN: 0615974376
ISBN-13: 978-0615974378

Printed in the United States of America.

The
Credo
Courses

TABLE OF CONTENTS

TABLE OF CONTENTS

SESSION #1

THE IMPORTANCE OF THE RESURRECTION OF JEUS

THE RESURRECTION OF JESUS

1. Deity of Jesus

2. Death of Jesus

3. Resurrection of Jesus

The Resurrection

- Center of NT Theology

- Center of NT Practice

The Beginning and the End of EVERYTHING

As long as we're sure that Jesus is the son of God, who died on the cross for our sins, and was raised from the dead... Christianity follows.

Two Strongest Evidences for Naturalism

1. Evolution

2. The Problem of Evil

There are More than 300 Verses in the New Testament that Refer to the Resurrection of Jesus

Resurrection Topic 1: Believers Will Be Raised Like Jesus

- Acts 4:2

- 1 Peter 1:3

Resurrection Topic 2: Grieving with Hope

- 1 Thessalonians 4:13-18

Current Scholarship Surrounding the Research Field of the Resurrection

- Since the mid-1970's, the field of theological studies has experienced a mild shift to the right.

Raymond E. Brown

- Major American name for NT studies, near the close of the 20th century

- *Introduction to New Testament Christology* (1994)

Where are we in Resurrection Studies?

- A similar shift has occurred

- More scholars today believe something really happened to Jesus after his death than those who do not.

The Preponderance of Evidence Says Jesus was Raised

Summary: Two Questions

1. Do we know the resurrection happened?

2. And if it did happen, how would it ground our major tenets of theology in practice?

A PRIORI OBJECTIONS, PART 1

THE RESURRECTION OF JESUS

Types of Objections

- A Posteriori: "after the data"

- A Priori: "before the data

A Priori Rejection vs. A Priori Objection

- A Priori *Objection*: a philosophical, or historical objection, which requires other foundational questions be answered before data can be considered

- A Priori *Rejection*: making a ruling that says data is wrong, or inaccurate before even hearing it

A Priori Objections: 3 Categories

1. Evidence

2. Laws of Nature

3. Epistemic Questions

David Hume

Miracle: **An event brought about by God, or an invisible agent**

A Priori Objections: 3 Questions

1. Do you have enough evidence?

2. Can I subsume the event you've claimed by expanding the laws of nature?

3. What do I do when I can't bridge the event you've claimed back to God?

Responding to A Priori Objections

Question: Do you have Enough Evidence?

Answer:

    A. Yes, I do.

- If the objection comes "before the data" there's no reason to show your hand of evidence.

More scholars today (in the field of Christology), believe something happened to Jesus after his death than those who believe nothing happened to Jesus

- 66% - 75% of scholars in this field believe in the empty tomb because there are now 23 arguments to support it

Responding to A Priori Objections

Question: Can I subsume the event you've claimed by expanding the laws of nature?

Answer:

A. You have a point concerning general miracle claims, but it will not work with the resurrection of Jesus

Responding to A Priori Objections

Question: Can I subsume the event you've claimed by
expanding the laws of nature?

Answer:

B. You cannot expand the laws of nature for one
person

Unlike every other resurrection story, Jesus does not
die again

TWO CLAIMS

- Jesus is the only founder of a major world religion who ever claimed to be God

- Jesus is the only founder of a major world religion who's believed to have been raised from the dead, in such a way as to not have to die again

Responding to A Priori Objections

Question: Can I subsume the event you've claimed by
expanding the laws of nature?

Answer:

C. Go ahead. Change the laws.

Saying, "Dead men don't rise, except for Jesus" says
exactly what the New Testament says

Summary: Responses to A Priori Objections 1 & 2

1. Evidence: We have more evidence than most Christians know about. We have more evidence than we NEED.

2. Laws of Nature: Changing them doesn't work for the resurrection of Jesus.

SESSION #3

A PRIORI OBJECTIONS, PART 2

A Priori Objection

A "before the data" objection that will destroy a case no matter what the evidence is

A Priori Objections 1 & 2

1. Do you have enough evidence?

2. If I expand the laws of nature, will the events you claim fall through the cracks?

Naturalism

- A worldview that states the natural world is all there is and that whatever one perceives, one gains knowledge of through scientific data

Evidence: Playing Offense

- Saying science is the best way to learn something is one thing-- saying science is the only way to learn something is quite another

Common Naturalist Claim

- No proposition is valuable unless science speaks on its behalf

<u>Response</u>

- The rule that states the chief or only evidence is scientific evidence is NOT scientific

- It cannot be tested by the scientific method

- It is based on faith

"Dead men stay dead, unless your name is Jesus," affirms exactly what the New Testament teaches...

A Priori Objection 3

- How do you trace a miracle back to God? (What name is inside your coat/ collar?)

Tough Question #1

<u>Christian Claim</u>: Jesus was raised from the dead; therefore, whatever he taught was true (because he's Lord); so, when he says we should follow him, we should listen.

- Does the same logic work with anyone other than Jesus?

Responding to Tough Question #1

- No one else in history fits into the same category as Jesus; there are no other resurrection accounts like his.

Tough Question #2

- Why should I believe in the resurrection over a mass hallucination, when the resurrection sounds more unlikely?

Responding to Tough Question #2

- It is NOT a choice between the only resurrection in history, or the only mass hallucination in history

- It is a choice between the only resurrection in history, or a series of FOUR of the only mass hallucinations in history

Tough Question #3

What if the disciples stole the body, died denying it, and it was the only time in history someone died for a known lie?

- Every time any of the apostles had a chance to deny Jesus for their lives, they chose death.

- This happened to Jesus followers at least 100 times in the early church!

Responding to the Naturalist Worldview

1. What if there's a God?

2.   What if miracles still happen today?

3.   What if there's an afterlife?

Why Should We Assume the Naturalist Worldview?

Evidence 2: Playing Offense Against the Naturalist

- When someone asks for evidence, propose a hypothetical alternative and ask them to give evidence for it

  - (I.e.) Jesus came from Venus

Summary: Bridging the Resurrection to God

1.   Is there a God?

2.   Do miracles still happen today?

3.   Is there an afterlife?

SESSION #4

PRINCIPLES
OF
HISTORIOGRAPHY

THE RESURRECTION OF JESUS

How do you Know if you Have a Good
Historical Argument?

How do you know when you come across data
that are trustworthy?

Important Note:

- Virtually no ancient Greco-Roman historian writes without recording miracles, supernatural omens, prophecies, etc.

Criteria of Authenticity:

- Like historians, NT scholars today apply a series of rules to texts to measure their historical accuracy

Important Features NOT Included Under Criteria of Authenticity:

1. Early Reports

2. Eyewitness Reports

Criteria of Authenticity:

1. Multiple Independent Attestation ("2 heads are better than 1")

The Jesus Seminar

- Leftist group of contemporary scholars who reject the deity and resurrection of the historical Jesus

- Once referred to as the "Barnum and Bailey" of NT scholarship

- In *What did Jesus Say?*, they claim having TWO independent sources for one of Jesus' sayings makes it immensely more likely that Jesus actually said it

Bart Ehrman

- Best known skeptical scholar in America

- Claims we cannot question certain events in Jesus' life because we have such a high number of independent attestations for them

Criteria of Authenticity

2. Dissimilarity/ Double Dissimilarity

   (I.e.) The Case of Jesus

   - If Jesus says something that neither a pre- Christian, Jewish scholar or the Early Church would have said, Jesus likely said it.

An Argument From Dissimilarity

1.   Jesus called himself the "Son of Man"

   •   "Son of Man" is a title of deity

   •   Neither Jews, nor the Early Church, referred to Jesus in this way

5 Gospel Sources

1. Mark + anywhere else = Mark

2. John

3. Matthew (only) = M

4. Luke (only) = L

5. Q (Alternate source to which Matthew and Luke refer)

   •   In how many of the 5 gospel sources does Jesus use the name "Son of Man?"

   - ALL FIVE

   •   In how many of the 5 gospel sources is Jesus displayed as a miracle worker?

   - ALL FIVE

Criteria of Authenticity

3. Embarrassment

   - Peter denied Jesus 3 times

   - James, the brother of Jesus, was a skeptic

4. Enemy Attestation

5. Coherence

   - When there are two similar events, one of which is backed by strong supportive evidence, they both are likely to have happened

6. Aramaic Substrata

   - Critics believe when Jesus uses Aramaic in the Gospels, it is the closest insight we have into his literal words

Scholars Introduce New Criterion

   - Why was Jesus crucified?

SESSION #5

METHODOLOGY: HOW DO WE USE HISTORIOGRAPHY IN APOLOGETICS

THE RESURRECTION OF JESUS

Two Methods:

1. The Reliability Method

2. The Minimal Facts Method

Reliability Method:

Top-down Argument: Umbrella

Main Idea: If we have a good text, everything under that text (all data found within it) is probably true

Reliability Method: Two Steps

1. Manuscript evidence.

   (We Have the Text)

2. Checks and balances to show authors' words were also accurate.

   (What the Text Says is Generally True)

Reliable Text Argument

Copied Well

▼

Factually True

▼

Inspired

Minimal Facts Method:

Bottom-up Argument: Brick Wall

Main Idea: Uses only data that is considered fact (highly probable) and is also affirmed by the vast majority of scholars

Minimal Facts Method: Two Characteristics

1.   Fact must be supported by multiple arguments.

    - (I.e.) Criteria of Authenticity

2.   The vast majority of scholars must accept the historicity of a fact because they find its supportive arguments convincing.

What Does it Mean for a Fact to be *Well-Attested* by the Vast Majority of Scholars?

How Many Scholars Make up the Vast Majority?

- Representative pool must be $\geq 90\%$

Minimal Facts Method:

- Only uses facts that the vast majority allows

- If facts aren't shared they are omitted

SESSION #6

APPROACHING SCRIPTURE

THE RESURRECTION OF JESUS

Approaching Scripture: Building on the <u>Minimal Facts Method</u> and Resolving Contradictions for the <u>Reliability Method</u>

If a skeptic doesn't believe in the Bible, it doesn't mean the Bible can't be effectively cited...

The Minimal Facts Argument

- Only uses the Bible as an ancient book of religious literature

Central Argument

- If the NT is inerrant ▶ Jesus has been raised from the dead

- If the NT is NOT inerrant, but only a good source for ethics and historical data ▶ Jesus has been raised from the dead

- If the NT is NOT inerrant, OR historically reliable, but only a book of ancient religious literature ▶ Jesus has been raised from the dead

Contradiction 1: Lists of Women who Went to the Tomb in the Gospels

- If the text _is_ wrong, what follows?

Crucial Point

- If the NT is only a book of ancient literature, that has more error than fact… it can still be argued that Jesus was raised from the dead.

Contradiction 2: Number of Angels found at the Tomb in the Gospels

- Matthew and Mark count 1 angel

- Luke and John count 2 angels

Contradiction 3: Paul's List of Jesus' Appearances in 1 Corinthians 15

3 Common Contradictions

1. Which women went to the tomb?

2. How many angels were there?

3. Does Paul's list of Jesus' appearances agree with the Gospels' list?

Responding to Contradiction 1: Which Women went to the Tomb?

Matthew: Mary, Mary

Mark: Mary, Mary, and Salome

Luke: Mary, Mary, and Joanna

John: Mary (Magdalene)

Context Considered: Mary, Mary, and Salome

Mark 15: 40-41 (NKJV):

"There were also women looking on from afar, among whom were Mary Magdalene, Mary the mother of James the Less and of Joses, and Salome, who also followed Him and ministered to Him when He was in Galilee, and many other women who came up with Him to Jerusalem."

Context Considered: Mary, Mary, and Salome

Luke 24: 1,10 (NKJV):

1 "Now on the first day of the week, very early in the morning, they, and certain other women with them, came to the tomb bringing the spices which they had prepared."

10 "It was Mary Magdalene, Joanna, Mary the mother of James, and

the other women with them, who told these things to the apostles."

Context Considered: Mary Magdalene (only)

John 20: 1-2 (NKJV):

"Now on the first day of the week Mary Magdalene went to the tomb early, while it was still dark, and saw that the stone had been taken away from the tomb. Then she ran and came to Simon Peter, and to the other disciple, whom Jesus loved, and said to them, "They have taken away the Lord out of the tomb, and we do not know where they have laid Him."

The Rule for Contradiction

- Two things cannot both be <u>and</u> not be at the same *time*, in the same *place*, in the same *manner*.

Responding to Contradiction 2: How many Angels were at the Tomb?

Matthew: 1 angel

Mark: 1 angel

Luke: 2 angels

John: 2 angels

Responding to Contradiction 3: Does Paul's List of Appearances Agree with the Gospels' List?

1.   Peter

2.   All the Apostles

3.   500 brethren

4.   James

5.   All the Apostles

6.   Paul (himself)

Crucial Point

- Responding to these "Contradictions" is only necessary for the Reliability Method

- It is <u>not</u> necessary for the Minimal Facts Method

SESSION #7

MINIMAL FACTS METHOD

THE RESURRECTION OF JESUS

Minimal Facts Method: What do the "Minimal Facts" Look Like on the Resurrection?

Minimal Fact 1: The Death of Jesus

- Jesus Died by Crucifixion

Three Best Known Skeptical Religious Scholars in America

- Bart Ehrman

- John Dominic Crossan

- Marcus Borg

Borg, Crossan, and Ehrman all affirm Jesus' Death by Crucifixion

Minimal Fact 2: Jesus' Central Teaching is the Kingdom of God and How to Get There

Minimal Fact 3: After Jesus' Death, his Disciples had Experiences that <u>they</u> Believed were Appearances of the Risen Jesus

Minimal Fact 4: An Apostle, named Saul of Tarsus, who on his way to Damascus, had an Experience that <u>he</u> believed to be an Appearance of the Risen Jesus

Minimal Fact 5: James was a Skeptic, who did not Believe until he met the Risen Jesus

Minimal Fact 6: The Disciples Despaired after the Death of Jesus

Minimal Fact 7: Early Proclamations of the Resurrection

Minimal Fact 8: The Resurrection was the Central Proclamation of the Early Church and remains the Central Proclamation of Christianity Today

Goals for Remainder of Course

1. Discuss the minimal facts data

2. Discuss current scholarship surrounding the data

"Top Tier" Minimal Facts

1. Jesus' Death by Crucifixion

2. Disciples had experiences that they believed were appearances of the risen Jesus

3. Saul of Tarsus (later Paul) converted to Christianity because he believed he had an experience with the risen Jesus

4. Early Proclamations of the Resurrection

SESSION #8

PREACHING BEFORE COMPLETION OF NEW TESTAMENT

THE RESURRECTION OF JESUS

Of What did the Earliest Preaching Consist Before the Very First NT Book was Written?

The Death of Jesus ~ 30 A.D.

What makes us think that the texts we have beginning in 50 A.D. are as accurate as the very first messages in 31 A.D.?

Is there anything we have that fills the gap between 30 A.D. and 50 A.D.?

- The Early Christian Creeds

For the purposes of this lecture, the words "creeds," "confessions," and "traditions" will be used synonymously

Scholarship today supports that up to 90% of Jesus' listeners were illiterate

How can we be sure that Jesus' message was properly passed on between 30 A.D. and 50 A.D.?

1. Jesus' earliest followers took notes (James D.G. Dunn)

2. Transmission of Oral Traditions (I.e.- Storytelling, parables, etc.)

Accuracy of Transmission: Oral Traditions

- Disciples passed on stories and short sayings in a condensed, memorable manner

- The NT is filled with texts (confessions, traditions, creeds) that have cadences or rhythms

Early Church Creeds: 1 Timothy 3:16

"Beyond all question, the mystery from
which true godliness springs is great:

He appeared in the flesh,
was vindicated by the Spirit,
was seen by angels,
was preached among the nations,
was believed on in the world,
was taken up in glory." (NIV)

Early Church Creeds: 2 Timothy 2:11-13

Here is a trustworthy saying:

If we died with him,
we will also live with him;
if we endure,
we will also reign with him.
If we disown him,
he will also disown us;
if we are faithless,
he remains faithful,
for he cannot disown himself.

Early Church Creeds: 1 Corinthians 11

"For I received <u>from the Lord</u> what I also passed on to you..."
(1 Cor. 11: 23)

Early Church Creeds: 1 Corinthians 15

"For what I received I passed on to you..."
(1 Cor. 15: 3)

Three Best Known Creedal Passages in NT

1. Communion Passage (1 Corinthians 11)

2. Gospel Passage (1 Corinthians 15)

3. Kenosis Passage (Philippians 2)

Early Church Creeds: Romans 10:9

"...That if you confess with your mouth the Lord Jesus and believe in your heart that God has raised Him from the dead, you will be saved." (NKJV)

Early Church Creeds: 1 Corinthians 15

"For what I received I passed on to you as of first importance..."
(1 Cor. 15: 3) (NIV)

The Gospel, as Defined in the NT

1. Deity (indicated by title)

2. Atoning Death

3. Bodily Resurrection

Consensus NT Position

Richard Bauckham:

- Paul received this (creedal) material most likely when he went up to Jerusalem, just 3 years after his conversion

Historical Timeline

- The Cross ~ 30 A.D.

- Paul's Conversion ~ 1.5- 3 years after the Cross

- Paul Goes to Jerusalem ~ 4.5- 6 years after the Cross

When did Paul receive the "material" for his NT definition of the gospel (Deity, Death, and Resurrection)?

- Approximately 5 years after the Cross

Bart Ehrman

- Claims the best place to get eyewitness material in the NT is from Paul's trip to Jerusalem to talk to Peter and James

Support from Galatians 2

- "...they added nothing to my message." (Gal. 2:6) (NIV)

Richard Bauckham, Jesus and the God of Israel (2008)

- Claims the earliest Christology of all is the highest Christology of all

SESSION #9

NATURALISTIC THEORIES: ALTERNATIVE EXPLANATIONS FOR THE RESURRECTION

THE RESURRECTION OF JESUS

Principle of Ockham's Razor

*   States the simpler theory is essentially the better theory

Historical Framework for Naturalism

*   Truth claims about Bible were challenged- Biblical Criticism (1700s)

*   Benedict Spinoza- Higher Criticism

- David Hume (1750s)

Historical Framework for Naturalism

- The Deists- England (1730s)

  - Deism- God created the world and then backed off (Watch-Maker Theory)

  - Rejected the authenticity of fulfilled prophecy and miracles

- Herman Samuel Reimarus- popularized the theory that the Disciples stole the body of Jesus (1760s)

- Swoon Theory- Jesus survived the cross

- German Liberalism (1799- World War I)

  - Friedrich Schleiermacher- *On Religion: Speeches to its Cultured Despisers* (1799)

Blows to Liberalism

- Karl Barth- *The Epistle to the Romans* (1919)

- Politics of World War I- deconstructed theories of philosophical idealism and progress

Rise of Naturalism (~1800-1820)

- <u>Naturalistic Theories</u>- if one can explain data by natural means rather than supernatural means, the explanation is simpler

Theories of Early (German) Liberalism

1. Jesus did not die on the Cross

   - Friedrich Schleiermacher

   - Heinrich Paulus (1825)

2. The Hallucination Theory

   - David Strauss (1835)

3. <u>Karl Theodor Keim</u> (1870)- Jesus died and was raised, but not bodily ("Jedi Jesus")

4. Christianity borrowed from other Ancient Religions

Five Major Naturalistic Responses to the Resurrection

1. The disciples stole the body

2. Someone other than the disciples stole the body

3. Jesus did not die on the cross

4. The disciples saw hallucinations

5. Christians borrowed theories from other ancient religious groups

SESSION #10

NATURALISTIC THEORY 1: THE DISCIPLES STOLE THE BODY

THE RESURRECTION OF JESUS

Five Major Naturalistic Responses to the Resurrection

1. The disciples stole the body (Fraud A)

2. Someone other than the disciples stole the body (Fraud B)

3. Jesus did not die on the cross

4. The disciples saw hallucinations

5. Christians stole the resurrection message from other ancient mythology (Copycat Theory)

Supernatural Alternative Theory for the Resurrection

6. "Jedi Jesus"- Jesus died and was raised, but not bodily

Biblical References: The Disciples Stole the Body

- Jewish Leaders appeal to Pilate to have a guard placed at the tomb

  - Matthew 27:62-65

- Jesus is risen and the guard is paid to report that the disciples stole the body

  - Matthew 28:5-15

Biblical References: The Disciples Stole the Body

- One of the earliest known alternative theories

- Almost considered historically uncritical

- Herman Samuel Reimarus

Problems with Fraud A: It Implicates the Disciples

- The Disciples did not get rich

- The Disciples did not gain position and prestige

- The Disciples were <u>willing</u> to die for what they believed to be true

Were the Disciples Martyred?

- We have reports to support that all twelve apostles were martyred for Christianity (Matthias in place of Judas)

- We have a second century source to support the martyrdom of John also

- <u>Problem</u>: We do not have early and eyewitness sources for many of the Disciples' martyrdoms

Of Peter, John, James, and Paul, we have early, first century dates for the martyrdom of 3 of them

1. Peter- Clement (95 A.D.)

2. Paul- Clement (95 A.D.)

3. James- Josephus (80s A.D.)

Problems with Fraud A: Skeptics would not have gotten involved if the Disciples had stolen the body

- Paul (Saul of Tarsus)

- James (the brother of Jesus)

Crucial Point

- The main reason the majority of skeptics reject this theory is because the Disciples could not have both stolen the body of Jesus and sincerely preached his message

SESSION #11
NATURALISTIC THEORY 2: SOMEONE ELSE STOLE THE BODY

THE RESURRECTION OF JESUS

Naturalistic Theory 2: Someone Other than the Disciples Stole the Body (Fraud B)

Review

- <u>Naturalistic Theory 1</u> - The Disciples Stole the Body (Fraud A)

- The main problem with Fraud A is that it implicates the Disciples

Problems with Fraud B: It Does Virtually Nothing, but Explain the Empty Tomb

Advantage of Fraud B

- When combined with the Hallucination Theory, it provides a cause for both Jesus' appearances <u>and</u> the empty tomb

Problems with Fraud B: It Does Not Negate the Resurrection on its Own

Popular Sub-Argument for Fraud B

<u>Kirsopp Lake</u>- women went to the wrong tomb
- Lake believed in the Resurrection ("Jedi Jesus")

Biblical References: Someone Other than the Disciples Stole the Body

- Mary Magdalene   ▶   John 20: 13-15
    - Mary thinks Jesus was taken
    - Mary mistakes Jesus for the gardener

Weaknesses of Fraud B

- It explains <u>nothing</u> but the Empty Tomb

- It does NOT negate the Resurrection on its own

SESSION #12

NATURALISTIC THEORY 3: THE SWOON THEORY

THE RESURRECTION OF JESUS

The Swoon Theory

- Jesus made it to the cross, but the cross did not kill him

Main Objection of the Swoon Theory

- The whole truth of Christianity relies on the word of a Roman soldier who knows nothing about medicine

What Medical Experts Say About Death by Crucifixion

- Dr. Hermann Moedder

    - Simulated crucifixion with male volunteers

    - Tied to hanging 2x4s, volunteers lost consciousness in a maximum of 12 minutes

- Death by crucifixion is essentially death by asphyxiation

- Asphyxiation can shut down the whole body due to oxygen deprivation in the cells

"On the Physical Death of Jesus Christ," JAMA (1986)

- Claims the spear would not have caused his death, but would have ensured it

- Claims Jesus died due to hypovolemic shock and asphyxiation

Responses to the Swoon Theory

1. The soldier did not have to know medicine, but rather only how to properly crucify someone

    - If the majority medical opinion is correct, crucifixion ends in death by asphyxiation

Common Argument for the Swoon Theory

- In Josephus' *Autobiography*, he claims that some have survived crucifixion

On Josephus' Claim

- Three of Josephus' friends were being crucified

- They were let down alive

- The crucifixion process was shortened

- No one was mistakenly let down alive

- Two of the three died anyway

Responses to the Swoon Theory

2.   Jesus' ankles were NOT broken because he was already dead

3.   Jesus was stabbed in the chest

    •   Gospel of John

    •   Roman source discusses practice of piercing the body to make sure a person is dead

4.   David Strauss' Critique

    •   The main problem with the theory is logical

    •   You can't get from "He didn't die on the cross" to "He's the crucified and risen Lord of the world"

    •   The theory argues a living Jesus, NOT a risen Jesus, which negates the Christian message

SESSION #13

NATURALISTIC THEORY 4: THE HALLUCINATION THEORY

THE RESURRECTION OF JESUS

Celsus

- Second century philosopher and opponent of Christianity

- First to articulate that Jesus' resurrected appearance was sensationalized (*Mary Magdalene*)

David Strauss

- Gave form to the claim that Jesus' disciples saw hallucinations of Jesus rather than an authentic appearance of his resurrected body

Problems with Hallucination Theory: Groups

- There is no non-anecdotal account of a mass hallucination in history (verified by Dr. Gary Sibcy)

What is a Hallucination?

- An experience created in the mind of an individual that is projected and perceived as real

Three Types of Perceptual Experiences

1. Hallucination- experiencing something for which there is no external referent

2. Illusion- experiencing something that is really there, but thinking it to be something else

3. Delusion- experiencing something that is not real as a result of some brain disfunction

Problems with the Hallucination Theory: Variety

1. Hallucinations are <u>subjective</u> events

    •   Some are more inclined to hallucinate than others, some are less inclined than others

2. To say that different types of people, in different environments, at different times <u>all</u> had the same hallucination would be highly unlikely

Problems with the Hallucination Theory: The Tomb

•   It is a closed tomb view

•   It requires another theory to explain why Jesus' tomb was empty

Problems with the Hallucination Theory: Influence

•   Hallucinations are not likely to transform lives

•   People can often be easily talked out of hallucinations

Problems with the Hallucination Theory: Paul & James

- It's unlikely that enemies and skeptics would hallucinate in the same way as those zealous for the faith

Problems with the Hallucination Theory: Review

1. Hallucinations do not occur in groups

2. Not everyone would have been hallucination dependent

3. The theory does not explain the empty tomb

4. Hallucinations do not normally change lives

5. Paul (enemy) & James (skeptic) would not have likely shared in the experience

Where can this theory be found in the Gospels?

- Luke 24: 36-39

SESSION #14
NATURALISTIC THEORY 5: COPYCAT THEORY

THE RESURRECTION OF JESUS

Christians Stole the Resurrection Message from Other Ancient Mythology (Copycat Theory)

Popular Claim for Copycat Theory

- There have been many living, or non-living mythical figures who were crucified and raised, and Christianity copied them

Three Forms of Legend/ Myth

1. Stories that keep expanding when retold

   - Luke 24:11

2. Dying and rising gods who never lived

  • The Cult of Isis

3. Figures tied to resurrection myths, who actually lived

  • Apollonius of Tyana, Sabbatai Zevi, etc.

Helmut Koester, Introduction to the New Testament Vol. 1 (1995)

• There is NO resurrection in the story of Isis and Osiris

• Isis is the hero of the story, not Osiris

Response to Myth Form 1

• Even according to skeptics like Bart Ehrman, the Church began teaching the resurrection of Jesus immediately after his death

The Key to Christianity

• It is NOT which myths were circulating during the early Church, but that it is historically reliable

• Both the disciples' claimed experiences with the risen Jesus and the empty tomb must be explained

Scholarship Today Says...

- There were NO crucified and risen savior figures before Jesus, mythical or otherwise

The Earliest Cases of Resurrection Myths Came <u>After</u> Jesus

- Adonis (2nd Century A.D.)

- Attis (3rd Century A.D.)

Examining Apollonius of Tyana

- Main source is Philostratus, *Life of Apollonius of Tyana*

  - Writes ~120 years after Apollonius

- Claimed to be an early form of the "novel" genre

- The stories are said to have come from one, Damis, a student of Apollonius

- According to dating within Philostratus' writing, Apollonius visits non-existent cities, non-existent kings, etc.

- There is no death of Apollonius recorded in Philostratus' work

- Philostratus claims Apollonius experiences apotheosis, not resurrection

Examining Sabbatai Zevi

- Sabbatai was captured by Muslims, who threatened to kill him if he did not tell his followers what they wanted him to

    1.   He is not the Messiah

    2.   They must convert to Islam

- When Sabbatai died his prophet, Nathan, claimed he was not dead, but only swooning

    - Sabbatai never returned

- There is an Empty Tomb story surrounding Sabbatai

Crucial Point

- There are NO crucified and risen saviors recorded in history before Jesus

SESSION #15

SUPERNATURAL ALTERNATIVE THEORIES

THE RESURRECTION OF JESUS

Karl Theodor Keim

- German professor who wrote, *Jesus of Nazareth* and the *National Life of Israel* (1867-1872)

- Refuted Strauss' Hallucination Theory

- Claimed that Jesus was really raised from the dead, but not bodily

- Keim introduced his supernatural alternative theory less than 10 years before the birth of Spiritism (England, 1880)

- Keim, who was a liberal scholar, simply dismissed the Empty Tomb Theory

- Jesus died, was raised, taken to heaven, and divinized

- Jesus, with God the Father, sent supernaturally manifested images of himself back to his disciples

- Jesus was NOT present

Hans Grass

- 20th Century, German Theologian

- Explains appearances as disembodied, glorified pictures where Jesus is present

- An improvement over Keim

- Claimed the images of Jesus that the disciples saw were disembodied, glorified pictures

- Jesus was present with them in spirit

Supernatural Theory 3

- The disciples saw "Post-death" visions of Jesus

- John Dominic Crossan takes a *natural* view of this theory, claiming the disciples had "post-death" visions of Jesus that were similar to hallucinations

Problems with the "Post-Death" Visions Theory

- It strips the Resurrection of its unique features

    - The exclusivity of Jesus is revoked

    - Jesus is no longer considered the only away to salvation

Common Feature of All Three Supernatural Alternative Theories

- Jesus appears in a NON- bodily manner

How Do We Know the Resurrection of Jesus was Bodily?

1. N.T. Wright, *The Resurrection of the Son of God* (2003)

    - Concludes that in the ancient world, Pagans, Jews, and Christians alike understood the Greek word "*anastasis*" (resurrection) to mean <u>bodily</u> resurrection

2. The empty tomb must still be explained

3. Mike Licona, *The Resurrection of Jesus: A New Historigraphical Approach* (2010)

   • Romans 8:11

   • Philippians 3:21

4. Skeptics like Gerd Lüdemann, John Dominic Crossan, and Dale Allison affirm that Paul's writings refer to a bodily resurrection

SESSION #16

CATEGORICAL PROBLEMS WITH NATURALISTIC THEORIES

THE RESURRECTION OF JESUS

Categorical Problem (1)

- 19th century German Criticism depends heavily on David Hume's critique, "Of Miracles" (1748)

- Hume was wrong!

George Mavrodes, "David Hume and the Probability of Miracles" (1998)

- In his article, "Of Miracles," David Hume claims we have <u>uniform</u> experience against <u>all</u> miracles (we no testimony to support miracles)

Mavrodes' Critique

- Hume's sample group was too small

- If his sample group had been expanded, miracle accounts would have been reported

- If Hume was wrong then 19th century German Liberalism and Naturalistic Theories were founded on his error

Categorical Problem (2)

- No single naturalistic theory explains all the data

- Compounding theories multiplies improbabilities

Categorical Problem (3)

- Liberal scholars competing for dominance in the 19th and early 20th centuries would introduce their own work with refutations of other scholars' work

  - Keim- refutes Hallucination Theory

  - Strauss- refutes Swoon Theory

There are two movements during this era that refute its naturalistic theories

- Liberals vs. Liberals

- Conservatives vs. Liberals

Categorical Problem (4)

- Most 20th century scholars reject the whole body of alternative naturalistic theories

    - (I.e.) Karl Barth

- Today, it is rare to find liberal scholars who affirm naturalistic theories

Categorical Problem (5)

- None of the naturalistic theories can explain the historical data

- The minimal facts (evidence) alone are enough to refute the naturalistic theories

SESSION #17

UNDERSTANDING THE MIND OF A SKEPTIC

THE RESURRECTION OF JESUS

Skeptical Platitude

- Extraordinary claims require extraordinary evidence

- If his sample group had been expanded, miracle accounts would have been reported

Response to Skeptical Platitude

- What is more extraordinary than a supernatural event that has only occurred one time in history?

- Jesus has been resurrected <u>never to die again</u>

Features of a Skeptical Mind (1)

- There is often an unwritten understanding among skeptics that truly *extraordinary* evidence is unattainable

- No amount of evidence will ever be enough

Features of a Skeptical Mind (2)

- Some skeptics do not find it necessary to provide an alternative naturalistic theory

- ANY naturalistic theory is more likely than the resurrection of Jesus

What Can We Do to Change the Skeptical Mind?

1. Provide some attainable evidence

2. Present alternative worldview perspectives

Thomas Nagel

1. Professor of philosophy at New York University

2. *Mind and Cosmos: Why the Materialist Neo-Darwinian Conception of Nature is Almost Certainly False* (2012)

Michael Ruse

- Philosopher of science at Florida State University

- Embarrassed by Richard Dawkins' display of atheism

SESSION #18

CHANGING THE SKEPTICAL MINDSET OF THE NATURALIST, PART 1

THE RESURRECTION OF JESUS

What Can Be Done to Change the Skeptical Mindset of the Naturalist?

Brooke Foss Westcott

- The antecedent probability against miracles is so high that even before dialogue begins, it is decided that miracles cannot be considered

- <u>Unless God exists</u>

Which topics, if perceived as true, would upset the probability structure for skeptics enough to give them rise to consider the resurrection?

Topic 1: New Logical Arguments for the Existence of God

1. The Kalam Cosmological Argument

   • William Lane Craig

2. The Ontological Argument

   • Alvin Plantinga, *God, Freedom, and Evil* (1974)

Topic 2: Fine Tuning Cosmic Constants in the Universe

1. The Ocean

2. Gravity

Topic 3: Intelligent Design

1. Michael Behe, *Darwin's Black Box: The Biochemical Challenge to Evolution* (1996)

2. William Dembski, *Intelligent Design: The Bridge Between Science and Theology* (1999)

- Reproductive organs would take millions of years to develop

- If nothing was guiding the development, how could reproductive organs evolve before first generations died out?

Topic 4: New Scholarship Supports that Jesus was a Miracle Worker

- Historical evidence reinforces that Jesus did many "miraculous" things like those found in the Gospels

Graham Twelftree

- NT Professor at Regent University

- *Jesus the Miracle Worker: A Historical and Theological Study* (1999)

- Concluded 22 of 29 miracle stories in the Gospels reflect events in the life of the historical Jesus

John Meier

- NT Professor at Notre Dame

- *A Marginal Jew: Rethinking the Historical Jesus, Vol. 2: Mentor, Message, and Miracles* (1994)

- Concluded 13 of 30 miracle stories in the Gospels reflect events in the life of the historical Jesus

If Jesus was a miracle worker why is the resurrection worth NO consideration?

Naturalist Response: The resurrection stands as a one of a kind event

Supernaturalist Counter: Jesus was also a one of a kind person

- Jesus is the only founder of a major world religion who ever claimed to be God

Topic 5: Jesus Predicted his Death and Resurrection

- Mike Licona, "Did Jesus Predict his Death and Vindication/ Resurrection?" *Journal for the Study of the Historical Jesus* (2010)

- Leans on historical criteria

SESSION #19

CHANGING THE SKEPTICAL MINDSET OF THE NATURALIST, PART 2

THE RESURRECTION OF JESUS

Three Categories that Lead the Naturalist to Consider the Resurrection

1. The Existence of God

2. The Existence of Miracles

3. The Existence of an Afterlife

Review: Topics Under Jesus as Miracle Worker

- Historical criteria provides evidence for his "miracles"

- Jesus performed exorcisms

- Jesus predicted his death and resurrection

Craig Keener

- *Miracles: The Credibility of the New Testament Accounts* (2011)

- Critiques David Hume's claim that human experience dictates a uniform case against miracles

- Documents thousands of evidenced miracle claim

Topic 6: If miracles are occurring today, they may have also occurred in Jesus' day

- Jesus may have been a miracle worker

- Jesus may have predicted his resurrection

- Jesus may have performed exorcisms

Crucial Point

- If we live in a supernatural world, it could be a world in which we need comparatively less evidence for the resurrection (because of the nature of the claim)

Topic 7: New Creedal Evidence Links the Preaching of 30 A.D. to that of 50 A.D.

- The creedal passage beginning in 1 Cor. 15:3 dates within 1-2 years of the cross

Topic 8: New Scientific Evidence on the Shroud of Turin

- Kenneth Stevenson and Gary Habermas:

  1. *Verdict on the Shroud* (1982)

  2. *The Shroud and the Controversy* (1990)

- Stevenson was present for the testing done in Turin in 1978

- Photos of the shroud yield images of teeth

- The image is backlit because of a force (radiation) carried through the body

- Dead bodies do not irradiate cloth

Topic 9: Evidence for Near Death Experiences

- Catalogued over 100 evidential near death experiences (Gary Habermas)

- As in cardiac arrest, people with no heart or brain function have given accounts of verifiable events that occurred while they were flatlined/ unconscious

- Near death experiences argue for the potentiality of an afterlife

Topic 10: Double- Blind Prayer Experiments

- Prayer is observed to test whether or not petitions made to God can yield results

- Often experiments aim to test whether or not an association can be made between prayer and healing

SESSION #20

EVIDENCE FOR THE DEATH OF JESUS

THE RESURRECTION OF JESUS

Skeptical Stance on the Death of Jesus

1. Bart Ehrman, *Did Jesus Exist?: The Historical Argument for Jesus of Nazareth* (2012)

    -   Claims skeptics who are NOT trained might doubt that Jesus died on the cross

    -   Counts 11 independent sources for Jesus' death by crucifixion

2. John Dominic Crossan (The Jesus Seminar)

    -   Claims the death of Jesus is as well-established as any fact in the ancient world

3.   Marcus Borg (The Jesus Seminar)

   •   Claims the fact that Jesus died (as a political rebel) is
          well-established

Important Note

- In keeping with the Minimal Facts Method, the NT is not used as
  an inspired source of God's Word

- It is used only as a book of ancient religious literature

Sources for the Death of Jesus (Ehrman)

- The Apostle Paul

- Mark

- John

- Matthew & Luke material

- Hebrews

- 1 Peter

- 1 Timothy (author unknown)

- Tacitus

- Josephus

- Gospel of Thomas

- Gospel of Peter

The Apostle Paul

- Ehrman claims the best support comes from Paul

- Well-educated

- Faithful zealot for Judaism (pre- conversion)

- Persecuted those who met & studied under Jesus

- Interviewed those who knew Jesus

Pauline Epistles Skeptics Consider Authentic

1. Romans

2. 1 Corinthians

3. 2 Corinthians

4. Galatians

5. Philippians

6. 1 Thessalonians

7. Philemon

Criteria of Multiple Attestation

- According to this criteria there is a wide body of evidence to support this claim

- 11-22 independent sources support the historicity of Jesus' death by crucifixion

Possible Archaeological Sources

- Shroud of Turin

- The Nazareth Decree

Other Source Criteria for the Death of Jesus

1. Multiple Forms

2. Eyewitness Testimony

3. Early Evidence

   - Paul's visit with James and Peter

   - Sermon summaries in Acts (1-5, 10, 13, 17)

Other Source Criteria for the Death of Jesus

4. Enemy Attestation

    - <u>Tacitus</u>- calls Christian belief a "mischievous superstition"

5. Embarrassment

    - Peter denied Jesus

    - James thought Jesus was mentally ill

    - The disciples hid for fear of the Jews

6. Aramaic Substrata

    - Jesus: "My God, my God, why have you forsaken me? (*Eloi, Eloi, lama sabachthani?*)

      - Points to the cross

SESSION #21

EVIDENCE FOR THE APPEARANCES OF JESUS

THE RESURRECTION OF JESUS

The Core of Resurrection Evidence

- N.T. Wright, *The Resurrection of the Son of God* (2003)

   1. The Appearances of Jesus

   2. The Empty Tomb

General Critical Consensus on the Appearances of Jesus

- The earliest Christians had real experiences that THEY believed to be appearances of the risen Jesus

Importance of the Appearances of Jesus

- If pre-Christian data on resurrected mythological gods was found, the appearances would still have to be explained

- Christianity is based on its earliest witnesses having experiences with what they believed to be the risen Jesus

- The evidence for this has been well-established for 150-200 years

Evidence that the Resurrection is Based on Experience, not Stories Retold

1.   Creedal texts in Paul's Epistles

     A)   Pre-Pauline creedal passages

          a.   Romans 1: 3-4

          b.   Romans 10: 9

          c.   Philippians 2

          d.   1 Cor. 8:6

          e.   1 Cor. 15:3-7

How Do We Know 1 Cor. 15 is Pre-Pauline?

- Paul, himself, states he received the information from another source

Paul's List of Appearances in 1 Cor. 15:3-7

1. Peter

2. James

3. Paul (himself)

4. The Twelve

5. All the Apostles

6. The 500 brethren

(CONTINUED) Evidence that the Resurrection is Based on Experience, not Stories Retold

2. The women Jesus appears to in the Gospels

3. Creedal texts in the book of Acts

4. Matthew (M)

5. Luke (L)

6. John

7.   Other NT writers

8.   Josephus

Creedal Texts in the Book of Acts

- Acts 1-5, 10 (Petrine Creeds)

- Acts 13, 17 (Pauline Creeds)

C.H. Dodd

- *The Apostolic Preaching and its Developments : Three Lectures with an Eschatology and History* (1936)

- Claims Luke worked Petrine and Pauline creeds into messages summarized in the book of Acts

Petrine Creed in Acts 10: 39-43

- Reports the Appearances of Jesus

  - Jesus appeared

  - The disciples saw him

  - Jesus ate and drank with the disciples

Creedal Texts in the Book of Acts

- Dated 30s A.D.

- Dated within 1-2 years of the cross

Review: Development and Significance of Creedal Passages

- Standardized for a largely illiterate population

- Standardized in a way that they could be easily memorized

- Processed with literary devices and cadences

- James D. G. Dunn

  - Claims messages were standardized within months of the cross

- Larry Hurtado, *How on Earth did Jesus Become a God?: Historical Questions about Earliest Devotion to Jesus* (2005)

  - Claims the resurrection message immediately follows the cross

Other Criteria Supporting Jesus' Appearances

- Enemy Attestation

  - The Guard's Report (Matthew 28)

- The placement of the Jewish leaders at the time

- The large number of Jewish priests that became believers (Acts 6:7)

- Early/ Eyewitness Testimony

SESSION #22

EVIDENCE FOR THE EMPTY TOMB

THE RESURRECTION OF JESUS

Arguments for the Empty Tomb

- Reports come from women in the gospels

- The Jerusalem Factor

- Multiple Attestation

- Enemy Attestation

First Century Attitude Toward Women in the Mediterranean World

- Women <u>were</u> allowed to testify in court

- The more important the claim, the less one would want a woman to testify on its behalf

- Such reports were not considered reliable

Why are women's reports the most important evidence for the Empty Tomb?

- Drawing from slightly different source material, all four gospels still tell the same story

- Women brought spices to anoint the dead body, which means no one believed Jesus would rise

- All four gospels say the women are the heroes of the story

Apologetic Point

- Decades later (60s- 90s A.D.), all four gospel writers make the women their chief witnesses for the Empty Tomb

- The only reason to do such a thing would be if it were true

- All the gospel writers agree on something that costs them to tell the story in that way

The Jerusalem Factor

- Jerusalem would be the worst place to proclaim the Empty Tomb message if it were not true

    - Jewish leaders

    - Roman soldiers

    - Pilate

    - Herod

Common Critical Response to the Empty Tomb Theory

- The disciples did not begin preaching until Pentecost (50 days after the alleged resurrection)

- After 50 days Jesus would have been unrecognizable, so if questioned the disciples could have denied it

Rebuttal

- Mike Licona and Gary Habermas, *The Case for the Resurrection of Jesus* (2004)

    1. Talked to two independent pathologists who claimed that even in a Middle- Eastern, spring climate, a body would not have been unrecognizable in 50 days

    2. The early Christian teaching is that the tomb was EMPTY

Multiple Attestation

- Of the four gospels, 3-4 of the Empty Tomb accounts are independently sourced

- An early sermon summary in Acts 13: 32-38 supports the Empty Tomb (Pauline)

- Bart Ehrman claims the passage predates the gospels (about 30s A.D.)

- The passage in 1 Cor. 15 progresses toward an inevitable empty tomb

  - Jesus died

  - Jesus was buried

  - Jesus rose again

  - Jesus appeared

N.T. Wright, The Resurrection of the Son of God (2003)

- For Pagans, Jews, and Christians in the ancient world, the Greek words *"anastasis"* and *"egeiro"* always concerned a bodily resurrection

SESSION #23

CONSTRUCTING A HISTORICAL TIMELINE

THE RESURRECTION OF JESUS

Exploring the Significance of Early, Eyewitness, and Empty Tomb Data

The Buddhist Scriptures

- Claims there are more Buddhist texts than there are texts for any other religion

- Claims Buddhism is not like Christianity

What Christians Have that Buddhists Do Not

- The words of their Lord

- The words of those who heard from their Lord

- The words of those, who heard from those, who heard from their Lord

What Christians Have that Buddhists Do Not

- The Death of Jesus (Ground Zero) ~ 30 A.D.

- Paul writes 1 Corinthians ~ 55 A.D.

Alternative Examples from History

1. Alexander the Great

   - None of the major works on Alexander were written less than 300 years after his death (~323 B.C.)

   - Biographies of Alexander (400- 450 years after his death)

     - Arrian- *The Anabasis of Alexander*

     - Plutarch- *Life of Alexander*

2. Buddha

- First extended sources come 300-500 years after his death

3. Emperor Tiberius

- First sources come ~ 80+ years after his death

- Tacitus

- Suetonias

When Did Paul Come to Corinth?

- We know from the NT (Acts 18:12), who the Corinthian leader was when Paul arrived

- His name has been found in a pavement inscription

- City leaders in Corinth only served 1 year terms

- Paul comes to Corinth (51- 52 A.D.)

- Writes 1 Corinthians a few years later

Where and from Whom did Paul Receive his Early Gospel Message?

- 1 Cor. 15:3- "For what I received I passed on to you as of first importance…" (NIV)

Paul Received his Early Gospel Message ~ 5 Years After the Cross (30 A.D.)

- Acts 1-9 claims Paul met Jesus between 1.5- 3 years after the cross (+3 years)

- In Galatians 1:17-18, Paul claims he spent 3 years in Arabia after his conversion (+5- 6 years)

- Afterwards, Paul goes up to Jerusalem to meet with Peter and James for 15 days

Crucial Point

- It matters less when Paul received the creeds and more when he received the substance of his gospel message

- This message is reflected in the book of Galatians

Galatians 2

- Gal. 2:1- Paul went back to Jerusalem (14 years later)

- Gal. 2:2- Paul shared, with Peter and James, the gospel he'd been preaching to the Gentiles

- Gal. 2:6- Peter and James added nothing to Paul's message

Crucial Point

- Paul hears the Gospel message at +5- 6 (after the cross)

- Peter and James had the material before Paul heard it

- It took time to form the message into cadenced creedal sayings

- All this data points to an early gospel message, consisting of the deity, death, and resurrection of Jesus

SESSION #24

APOLOGETICS, PART 1: BUILDING A BRIDGE FROM MIRACLES TO CHRISTIANITY

THE RESURRECTION OF JESUS

How do we know that because miracles occur, Christianity is true?

Three Arguments

1. The definition of "miracle"

   - There is a special connection between miracle and message

2. Jesus taught of/ through his miracles in general

- Jesus taught in particular of/through his resurrection

3. When the Early Church saw Jesus' resurrection, it pointed his followers to believe Christianity was true

Classical Definition for Miracle (David Hume)

- A violation of a law of nature brought about by God, or some invisible agent

New Testament Term for Miracle

- **Signs**- "pointers"- point to things beyond themselves

  - Often refer to power

  - Power is what is needed to bring signs about

Satan Can Perform Some Miracles

- **Revelation 13**

  - The image points to God's enemies (Satan, Antichrist, etc.)

  - Even for enemies of the gospel, miracles point beyond themselves to the truth of something

Jesus and General Miracles: Mark 2:1-12

- Jesus heals a paralytic

- Jesus first forgave the man of his sins

- <u>Teachers of the Law</u>- "...Who can forgive sins but God alone?" (Mark 2:6 NIV)

- <u>Jesus</u>- "'I want you to know that the Son of Man has authority on earth to forgive sins.' So he said to the man, 'I tell you, get up, take your mat and go home.'" (Mark 2:10-11)

Jesus and the Resurrection Miracle: Matthew 12 & 16

- Jesus points to the sign of the prophet Jonah

  - The sign points to Jesus' resurrection

  - The resurrection shows he is the Son of God

Jesus and General Miracles: Luke 7: 18-22

- <u>John's Disciples</u>- "When the men came to Jesus, they said, 'John the Baptist sent us to you to ask, Are you the one who is to come, or should we expect someone else?'" (Luke 7:20)

- <u>Jesus</u>- "So he replied to the messengers, 'Go back and report to John what you have seen and heard: The blind receive sight, the lame walk, those who have leprosy are cleansed, the deaf hear, the dead are raised, and the good news is proclaimed to the poor.'" (Luke 7:22)

- When the disciples ask how they are to know Jesus is the Messiah, he points to his miracles

The Resurrection Points to the Fact that Christianity is True

- Acts 2:22 (Peter)

    - Jesus' resurrection displayed that he was approved (by God)

- Acts 17 (Paul)

    - God commanded the world to repent through Jesus

    - Proof is found in God's raising Jesus from the dead

- Romans 1:3-4 (Paul)

    - The resurrection is sufficient to show that Jesus is Lord, Messiah, and Son of God

Crucial Point

- The God of the universe had to be involved for Jesus to have been raised from the dead

    - Satan could not have (it was a creation miracle)

    - Jesus could not have raised himself

- God raised him to show that he approves Jesus' message

SESSION #25

SESSION #25

APOLOGETICS, PART 2: ESTABLISHING A CONNECTION BE- TWEEN THE RESUR- RECTION AND THE EXISTENCE OF GOD

THE RESURRECTION OF JESUS

Apologetic Methodology: Two Schools of Thought

- Classical View

- Evidential View

Classical Apologetics: Two Steps

1. Establish that God exists

2. Establish that the God who exists is the Christian God

Evidential Apologetics: One Step

1. The miracle that establishes Christianity also establishes that God exists

Classical View: Prospective Argument

A. God comes before the resurrection, so evidence for his existence must come first

B. If God exists then his attributes would be required for the resurrection of Jesus to have occurred

Some Arguments for the Existence of God

*   Kalam Cosmological Argument

    *   Anything that begins to exist has a cause

    *   The universe began to exist

    *   Therefore, the universe has a cause

- Transcendental Argument

  - Thinking would be impossible without a preexisting logical structure, which would require a designer (God)

Evidential View: Retrospective Argument

- Begins with the resurrection and reasons back to the being (God) that had to preexist the event in order to cause it

- Jesus' Claims + The Resurrection = Verification of Claims

Claims Confirmed by Jesus' Resurrection

- He does miracles

- He predicts the future (his death and resurrection)

- He forgives sin

- He is deity

- Having faith in him or not, determines where one spends eternity

- He not only brings the Word of Life, but he also is the Word of Life

SESSION #26

WHO DID JESUS THINK HE WAS?: ESTABLISHING THE DEITY OF CHRIST

THE RESURRECTION OF JESUS

Important Acknowledgement

- Nowhere in any of the Gospels does Jesus say, "I am God."

Important Acknowledgement

1. Son of God

2. Son of Man

Strongest Gospel Reference for the Deity of Christ: Mark 14: 61-64

"…Again the high priest asked him, 'Are you the Messiah, the Son of the Blessed One?' **'I am,'** said Jesus. **'And you will see the Son of Man sitting at the right hand of the Mighty One and coming on the clouds of heaven.'** The high priest tore his clothes. 'Why do we need any more witnesses?' he asked. 'You have heard the blasphemy. What do you think?' They all condemned him as worthy of death." (NIV)

Claims Jesus Made Before the High Priest: Mark 14:62

1. "I am" (the Christ, the Son of God)

2. "You will see the 'Son of Man'"

3. (The Son of Man will be) "coming on the clouds"

4. (The Son of Man will be) "sitting at the right hand of God"

Claims Jesus Made Before the High Priest: Mark 14:62

- Some hold it is a title of humanity (as it is used in the Book of Psalms)

- Jesus does not use "Son of Man" as a title of humanity because the High Priest clearly does not interpret what he says this way

- In Mark 14:63, the High Priest proclaims Jesus a blasphemer

Claim 3: "Coming on the Clouds"

- According to Old Testament Theology, this refers <u>always</u> and <u>only</u> to Jehovah

- Only God "comes on the clouds"

Claim 4: "Sitting at the Right Hand of the Mighty One (God)"

- This means Jesus claims he will share the throne of God

General Exegetical Consensus on Mark 14: 61-64

- Darrell Bock, *Blasphemy and Exultation in Judaism: The Charge Against Jesus in Mark 14: 53-65* (2000)

- Scholars like N.T. Wright, Craig Evans, and Darrell Bock agree that the greatest "blasphemy" was Jesus' claiming to share the throne of God

References to Jesus as "Son of God"

1. <u>Mark 13:32</u> "But about that day or hour no one knows, not even the angels in heaven, nor the Son, but only the Father."

   - NT scholar, Donald Guthrie- says this is surely an authentic claim because of how embarrassing it is

2. <u>Matthew 11:27</u> "All things have been committed to me by my Father. No one knows the Son except the Father, and no one knows the Father except the Son and those to whom the Son chooses to reveal him."

   - Early source- material found in Matthew and Luke, but not Mark, demonstrates an independent source (Q) earlier than Mark

2. <u>Mark 14: 36</u>

   - Jesus refers to God as "Abba"

     - Personal, familial title for The Father (not quite "daddy")

Biblical References to "Son of Man"

1. Book of Psalms- refers to "human being"

2. Ezekiel- refers to a prophetic figure

3. <u>Daniel 7: 13-14</u> "In my vision at night I looked, and there before me was one like a **son of man, coming with the clouds of heaven.** He approached the Ancient of Days and was led into his presence. He was given authority, glory and sovereign power; all nations and peoples of every language worshiped him. His dominion is an everlasting dominion that will not pass away, and his kingdom is one that will never be destroyed."

- Daniel 7 speaks of a preexistent divine figure, who is not the Father (sent by the "Ancient of Days")

- Good memorizing Bible: ESV, KJV, NET

First Century Jewish Publications Illuminate the "Son of Man' Figure in Daniel 7

- In works like 1 Enoch & 4 Ezra:

  - The "Son of Man accepts worship and shares God's throne

How Do We Know Jesus Meant "Son of Man" in the Lofty Sense?

- In his recorded ministry, Jesus paraphrases Daniel 7:13-14 when referring to himself

Two Reasons to Believe Jesus Called Himself the "Son of Man"

1. 5 of 5 Gospel sources confirm it

2. Criterion of Dissimilarity

    •   Jews did not apply the "Son of Man" title to Jesus

    •   "Son of Man" is Jesus' favorite title for himself and it is not recorded once in any NT epistle

SESSION #27

GROUNDING THEOLOGY, PART 1

THE RESURRECTION OF JESUS

Using the Resurrection to Confirm the Teachings of Jesus

Logical Progression

- Jesus has been raised; therefore, his teachings are true

- To know what is true is to know what Jesus taught

On What Grounds Do Christians Believe that The Bible is the Word of God?

- <u>Primary Evangelical Argument</u>- The book (Scripture) is reliable and the reliable book teaches that it is itself inspired; therefore, the book is inspired

- <u>Resurrection Argument</u>- Jesus accepted the inspiration of Scripture and Jesus was raised from the dead; therefore, Scripture is inspired

How Did the Early Church Confirm Jesus' Teachings?

- The NT clearly argues that by raising Jesus from the dead, God is confirming Jesus' message

Jesus Argued that his Miracles and his Resurrection Confirmed his Message

- Mark 2: 1-12

    - Jesus forgives sins and confirms his authority with a healing miracle

- Matthew 12 & 16

- Jesus points Jewish leaders to the sign of the prophet Jonah (the resurrection)

The Early Church Argued that Jesus' Resurrection Confirmed his Message

1. <u>Acts 2: 22-24</u>- Peter says Jesus was approved because he was raised

2. <u>Acts 17: 16-34</u>- Paul says the man Jesus has called the world to repent on God's authority because he was raised

3. <u>Romans 1:3-4</u>- Jesus showed himself to be Lord, Son of God, and Messiah (Christ) because he was raised

4. <u>1 Corinthians 15</u>

   a. (vv. 1-2): Whatever one does with Jesus determines where one spends eternity

   b. (vv. 12-15): If Christ has not been raised, the Apostles' preaching, witnessing, and faith are in vain (ungrounded)

   c. (v. 17): If Christ has not been raised, faith is futile

   d. (v.18): If Christ has not been raised, those who died in Christ have died in vain (are lost)

   e. (v. 19): If Christ has not been raised, we are of all men most miserable (to be pitied)

   f. (v. 20): **"But Christ has indeed been raised from the dead, the firstfruits of those who have fallen asleep"**

SESSION #28

GROUNDING THEOLOGY, PART 2

THE RESURRECTION OF JESUS

Grounding Theology, Part 2: Jesus is the Key to the Afterlife

Passages on Believer's Resurrection and the Afterlife

1. <u>John 14: 19</u>- Jesus says, "Because I live, you will live also"

2. <u>1 Cor. 6:14 / 2 Cor. 4:14</u>- Paul says God raised Jesus from the dead and will, therefore, raise his believers also

3. Phil 3:21- Paul says God will change our lowly bodies to be like Jesus' glorious body

4. 1 John 3:2- John says we shall see Christ as he is and we shall be like him

Two Arguments

1. Indirect Argument ("Around the Block")

    - Jesus says "something," and he was raised from the dead; therefore, it is confirmed true

        - (I.e.)- Jesus says there is an afterlife, and he was raised from the dead; therefore, it is confirmed true

2. Direct Argument ("Don't Miss the Forest for the Trees")

    - Because of the unique features of the resurrection itself, truth is established

        - (I.e)- The resurrection itself establishes the realm of an afterlife; therefore, that is the afterlife in which believers will live

What Does it Mean to Say the Disciples Saw the Risen Jesus?

- The disciples saw the light of heaven shining down

- The disciples saw walking, talking eternal life

Jesus' Number One Message was the Kingdom of God and How to Get There

Jesus Predicts the Kingdom of God

- For some, the "Kingdom of God" has come to mean something that happens after one's own death, or after Jesus returns

- Jesus actually said more about the present phase of the Kingdom (now) than the future phase (when he returns)

Word Studies: Eternal Life & Immortality

- Eternal Life- (I.e.) John 3:16

    - Greek (aionios)- means life to the end of the age, in the next age

        - Refers primarily to the quality of life one will live

        - Refers secondarily to quantity of life one will live

- Immortality (I.e.) 1 Cor. 15: 53-54

    dRefers primarily to quantity of life

        - Refers secondarily to quality of life

GROUNDING CHRISTIAN PRACTICE: APPLICATIONS BASED ON THE RESURRECTION

THE RESURRECTION OF JESUS

Applications Based on the Resurrection

The Resurrection and Christian Ethics

1. <u>1 Cor. 15: 32</u> "...If the dead are not raised, let us eat and drink for tomorrow we die"

- Paul seems to say that if Christ has not been raised, Christian ethics are ungrounded

The Resurrection and Giving to the Poor

- 1 Cor. 15:58 "Therefore, my beloved brethren, be steadfast, immovable, always abounding in the Lord, knowing that your labor is not in vain in the Lord" (NKJV)

- 1 Cor. 16:1 "Now concerning the collection for the saints…"

  - Take care of the poor

  - Reinforces Jesus' call to "love your neighbor as yourself"

- Galatians 6:10 "Let us do good to all, especially to those who are of the household of faith"

  - Reinforced in 1 Cor. 16 and 2 Cor. 8 when Paul takes up a collection on behalf of poor believers

The Resurrection and Heavenly Rewards

- 1 Cor. 3: 8 "…each will receive his own reward according to his labor"

THE RESURRECTION OF JESUS

THE RESURRECTION OF JESUS

The Resurrection of Jesus: Restoring and Securing a Reliable Faith in Christianity

1 Corinthians 15: 58

"Therefore, my beloved brethren, be steadfast, immovable…"

Frightening Statistics to Acknowledge

- Anywhere from 60-93% of young people who have gone away to secular schools, testify that they have walked away from their faith

- A follow-up book has been written, which claims most of these who have walked away from their faith end up coming back to it in their 30s

Two Problems

- Not everyone who leaves the faith comes back

- Those who come back have lost 10-15 of their most productive years, which could have been used for the Lord

What Would a Faith Look Like that Leaves us "Steadfast" and "Immovable?"

Three Causes as to Why People Slide into Doubt

1. <u>Peer Pressure</u>- secular professors, friends, etc.

2. <u>Sin</u>- leads people to redefine God in order to fit their preferences

3. <u>Emotional Reasons</u>-

   - People blame God for things that happen to them

   - If people cannot fix problems on their own, God is at fault

How Does People Walking Away from the Faith Relate to Paul's Message in 1 Cor. 15?

- <u>Admonition</u>- Because the resurrection has occurred, <u>do not</u> fall away

- The resurrection can be used to help strengthen those who feel pressured to walk away from the faith

Most People Walk Away from the Faith for Non-Factual, Non-Scholarly Reasons

- Because scholarly reasons are considered reputable, they are used to hide non-scholarly reasons (pressure, sin, emotion, etc.)

Nothing Disproves Christianity Except:

1. If Jesus is not the Son of God

2. If Jesus did not die for our sins

3. If Jesus was not raised from the dead

Crucial Point

- As long as Jesus is the Son of God, he died on the cross for our sins, and was raised from the dead...Christianity follows

- In these core tenets, our evidence is at its very strongest!

Christian Faith

- Grounds the facts

- Balances the emotional life

- Gives believers vision for the future

1 Corinthians 15: 55-57

"'O Death, where is your sting?

O Hades (grave), where is your victory?'

The sting of death is sin, and the strength of sin is the law. But thanks be to God, who gives us the victory through our Lord Jesus Christ." (NKJV)

ALL COURSES & RESOURCES:
CREDOCOURSES.COM

Made in the USA
Columbia, SC
16 February 2020

87901977R00104